The

sites.google.com/view/miriamrice/home

@miriams.art @poeteac

ISBN: 9781790834938

To my parents who taught me the importance of empathy

One of the most beautiful facets of art is its capacity for being an emotional outlet. When my heart feels heavy, and talking to loved ones is no longer therapeutic, I turn to art.

I found refuge in my pen, writing in my freshman English journal:

> "I feel deeply. I cope well with anger, annoyance, and disappointment, but at times I struggle with sadness. I am a happy person. I savor life like it is a ripe fruit, but sometimes the fruit is rotten. Why can't I throw rotten fruit away? I dwell on how it could have been sweet. I fixate on what could have been rather that what is-- which is an unhealthy. Possibility is addictive, reality sobering. When I am living under a cloud of sadness, I tend to cave into my introversion and curl away from people and into myself. I force myself to drown in the rain until I learn to swim."

I share my tender underbelly, my poetry, because scribbled in the margins of my ninth-grade journal, my teacher wrote-- 'You're quite the poetic voice.' His comment encouraged me to write poetry and was the impetus for this book.

Meaningful poetry is vulnerable because susceptibility is power. For my book to have an impact, my voice must be raw. So, my dear reader, I share swells of sadness that grappled me until I had to write to relieve them. I grouped these poems of emotional growing pains in the section titled 'Flow.' Like the ocean, our seemingly stable lives cycle between lows and highs. Emotions rise like a violent flow bashing the shore.

Then the tide ebbs. Fury recedes into serenity. Writing to cope with intricate and intense feelings, most work from my early teens reflects the 'flow' of life. But I have come to love poetry not only as a coping mechanism, but a celebration of beauty. The section 'Ebb,' largely influenced by my time in India, observes life's temperate recession.

Contents

Flow

I sip a cocktail of dull apathy and excessive empathy. I struggle with solidifying a future and living in the moment. I dream with my head in the clouds, but my feet planted firmly to the earth. I crave love but suppress it; it is a reverie I do not want reality to shred. Am I a dichotomy? No—I am more muddled than black and white. Am I gray? Or a spectrum of color?

My flushed arm lifts,
her black arm lifts too.
I walk on the sidewalk,
she trails behind me
clipping at my feet.
Am I the puppet master
because I control her movement?
Or have I no control since
I'm helplessly attached?

-*My Shadow*

Dear Hemingway; how do I condense my words into marble?

He dips his hands in yolk-yellow acrylic
And paints his canvas backpack
With scrambled handprints.
His hands like pitter-pattering seagull feet stomping.
How I wish I could poach his apathy for convention!
Unable to muster the courage, I swish my paintbrush
Back and forth like a complacent buttercup in the breeze.

-Restricted

St. Ive's Sea Salt Exfoliating body wash and
A spritz of Chanel I stole from my mom's bedroom,
The smell of which, makes me feel like
She is by my side although she is continents away.

-I Miss You

Miriam Rice

Woah!
The worry
The woe
Of being
Swept
Under the
Undertow!

16

y

I do not expect you to memorize me
Like a sailor internalizes the constellations—
But you cannot locate the North Star.

He is not angry.
He is protective.
Like a wounded animal
Lashing out in pain,
Unable to recognize
Someone trying to help.

The valley of indecision
Sinks into the shadow of its shame.
The watersheds swirl with
Sinister ink beneath the concrete.
I must escape—but
When I try to evade the swell,
I look up and see a night sky as
Dark and faded as me.

How do you rekindle the frenzied lamp
When the last drop of kerosene has burned?

-*Empty Relationships*

Sullen sunken souls
Sit silently steeping.
Solemn sighs slip.
Stress suffocates.
Slumber seduces.
Soft saffron sun sizzles.
Sitting students simmer.

-*School*

I remember as a young child, my mother gently nudged me awake. I was crying and mumbling Korean. My tongue aimlessly formed words that my ears did not comprehend. My lips trembled in grief for the loss of a beloved world they once embraced, now rusted like a bicycle in the rain. My tongue searched the cavity of my mouth for a word— a pedal— purged from my memory. Oh, the deep agony of not remembering something you once knew!

Do not offer yourself to people
Who ignore you like the veggie platter
At a Super Bowl party.

I am your tupperware
of neglected leftovers
forgotten in the fridge.

-*Faded Fling*

You are saturated with
the mask of sweetness—
tempting but deadly.
I am not a mindless fly.
I will not wander into
your greedy mouth.

-*Venus Fly Trap*

My heart is a gray,
Scabbed seabed.
There is not a drop of
vitality in my blood.
The fish rot.
They fester in the
bowl of my stomach;
Their flesh melting,
their carcasses shriveling.
I am a barren wasteland
that my soul is confined to.
The last drop of water
Has dried from my eye.
All I see is red.
All I feel is burning.

-Heartbreak

Words sit on the back of my tongue
like a kid at the top of a slide.
Afraid to fall they
clasp the handlebar and
look regretfully down
at the daunting ground.

My mother tells me: the baby that does not cry does not eat.

-*Speak Up*

Feeling bleh—
A sheep in a herd of
monochromatic
wooly coats.

-*What Ewe've Become*

You don't look at me the way you did before.
You don't look at me at all.
Today I caught a striking glimpse of the animosity that stirs in your skull.
Who planted that angry weed of hatred?
Who was the rash gardener who let bitter dandelions ravage my petaled memory?

-Am I the Gardener?

Driven mad by the fluorescent light,
A stink bug flits around my room.
It rams into the ceiling and walls.
I see how intangible desire
Makes the stink bug masochistic,
So how do I believe in heaven?

Miriam Rice

Break the tension;
pop the soda can
and gulp it down.

My God you are handsome—
like a ripe red mango,
Plump and saccharine.
How tantalizing that
You are just out of reach!

He stares at me through a curtain of blonde hair
Flopped over his brow.
My earthy features dig into his.
We seem starkly different,
But time will melt our appearances until one day
We reflect each other like snow reflecting clouds.
Our mildewed eyes will see similarities—
Our white heads, yellowed teeth, and hollowed cheeks.

-*We Are Flesh and Bone.*

A voice as flashy as the golden ring
Wrapped like a serpent 'round its finger.
It suffocates the room, asserting its dominance.
It is disgusting how it murders
And believes such malice is an act of a god!

Hippopotamus eyes peeking out
From their headwraps
Flood the streets.
Dear protesters,
How will you throw corruption
Out the swamp
When you have no hands?

"Mother do fish know what rain is?"
"No baby," she says, "fish can't tell if it's sunny or pouring."

I am sorry I didn't realize I was a fish, too engulfed in waters swirling around me to see a storm brewing on the horizon. If I had seen it, I would have swum to shore. I didn't. Now we are a drift log lodged in the sand.

You ask how two squares cut from the same cloth can be so different.

Look at the night sky bejeweled with stars. They are made of the same gaseous molecules. Hung side by side like diamond earrings they seem mere inches apart—but look deeper and you'll see they are separated by lifetimes.

How do I accept all of you?
The parts that drive me up a wall like a frantic spider?
The parts that tear me limb from limb?
The parts that make me burn?

Children gape at skyscrapers.
They marvel at the marble pillars
And glass windows
Reflecting the bustling city.
Like guppies on land
They flail their way into the
Tower and swim to the top.

Adults look down,
Peering out dull glass.
They see deserts of burnt rooftops
Stained in bourbon and rum.
The cars and people they once admired
Are ants to step on.

*U*nless we strengthen our trust
*S*he will wither to dust,
*A*shen lady liberty ravaged by rust.

She thinks she is a desert.
She looks in the mirror
And sees barren dunes
In the curve of her
Breast, belly, and hip.
Stretch-marks run
Over the dunes
Like tear stains of
A sizzled delta.
She has obsessed
Over the surface
Without realizing
She is an oasis
With vital currents
Pulsing within!

-Dig Deeper

The chameleon woman does not exist.
She is an amorphous clump of matter—
Atoms with no separation of self and other.
The molecules of her body and the air are indistinguishable.
She is nothing and everything at once.
She is the air filling people's lungs,
Assuming their identity as she loses herself.

.

Ebb

It is a full bladder tugging me out of bed at midnight.

-The Necessity to Write

I grab my pen and the ocean of emotion that swells in the bay
of my fingertips flows.

His eyes held an emotion I had never seen in him—
vulnerability. He is characteristically strong-willed but in that
moment the fire in his eyes was so blue it was like rippling
water.

Pull me under sheets
of ocean waves.
Soak my sunken soul.
With sand,
cover me,
shelter me.
Make me into a
sand castle and
reside in me.

-*To My Lover*

Snow covers the ground—
Powdered sugar on a doughnut.
I want to devour it—
To taste the crisp winter air in my lungs,
And feel the snowflakes kiss my cheeks.

-Winter Bliss

Some say space is the last frontier, but
Every stranger is an unexplored continent.

Frost said nothing gold can stay
But I wake up each day
To golden sun rays.

Their gentle caress makes me believe,
Although they leave,
Tomorrow they'll heave.

Eternally cutting through the gray,
They chase the clouds away,
And keep the pain at bay.

The fleeting feeling of fingers on my lip,
His flightful comment about how soft they are,
The image of kissing him rumbling by like a bullet train,
Flushing me with its force as it barrels down the tracks,
The blissful comfort,
The soft breaths mingling,
The rise and fall of his chest…

-*It Is Hypnotizing.*

Like the last sip of tea,
Our final memories
Were the sweetest.

Soft cotton candy skies,
Rain—Gaia's gentle cries.
Most, thick, humid air,
Weighed by Earth's despair.
Bugs come out to play,
Only on rainy days.
The sun beats down.
It burns and browns.
There is peace in rain,
It washes away pain.
It gives life to the dead,
A voice to words unsaid.
It seems so loud yet
It is quiet with regret.
Soft cotton candy skies,
Mother Nature is by my side.

Crown me and call me by my middle name.
Today I feel like Queen Elizabeth.

Wearing their crowns of dreadlocks,
The kings of the night
Perch upon their trash-can thrones
Smoking blunts as they lean back
And caw.

-The Ravens of New York City

I'm a seamstress
Hemming Hemingway
Into untailored prose.

Hermanita, never lose your trumpet laughter!
Never silence the Miles Davis in your throat
Because it is the most gorgeous sound I have ever heard.

When you wrap me
In your arms
And buck-toothed grin
And call me mi amorita,
I am at home.

-Home Is Feeling Not a Place.

Shower to clean the body,
Swim in the ocean to clean the soul.

Hammock snoozes in the paradise of muses
An iguana scutters by where I lie,
Limbs row up the palm to shade and calm.
I breathe in the ocean salt—sweet as malt.

-Present in the Present

Not the vibrant palette of this floral dress
Nor the tangerine stained-glass sky
Nor the velvet salad of watercress,
Nor the peach cream silk of my thigh
Can compare to the psychedelic kaleidoscope
Of a mind brimming with unbridled hope.

On a Claritin-clear day
While I float in the ocean,
I peer into the vast blue sky
And dive into it.
The world flips on itself
Ad suddenly I am
A pelican in the sky
Spreading its wings
To swoop down and clip the water.

-Flying

I will cradle you to my chest
So you are swaddled in
The comfort of rhythmic breath
Pulling and collapsing
Like the beat of the ocean.
Listen to my heart
Like a conch shell,
Pressing your ear to my rib.
Let go of what drags you
And sink into my arms.

-I Am Here for You.

You are tough to crack.
Your husk is a sheltering hut.
Open to the friendship you lack,
You'll be free from this isolated rut.

-Dear Coconut

Rhythm grabs my hips
And pulls me flush against its melody.
Together we sway stress away
Until we float on notes.

From the darkness,
An orchestra of rhythmic rain
And bellowing birds.
Dawn sets in.
Feet shuffle and
Meditations bells ring
As the ashram awakens like spring.

-Morning in Chennai

I am surrounded by unfamiliar—
Foreign tongues and bucket baths.
But I've never felt such love—
Radiant smiles and belly laughs.

A thousand souls sunk in silence
Purifying their hearts of violence.
Deep, deeper, deepest they dive
Into their minds, busy as bee hives.
Until, like a calm morning lake,
No ripples just glass—the true self awakes.

Whooping birds
Buzzing flies
Not a word
In paradise.
Cold marble floor
Caress of breeze,
Wealthy and poor
Leaves of the same tree.

Is love attachment?
No. Love is letting go for the better.
Love is savoring each moment
Out of respect for its impermanence.
Insecure love is obsession—
The inability to see beyond selfish desire.

Sit in the driver's seat of your body—
You, the radio, and the open road.
Trust yourself to steer.
Do not fear the inevitable destination.
Take ahold of your life and buckle in!

A moment before we are free—
Lips brimming with glee.
Ah what joy! Pure as ghee,
To blossom like a cherry tree.
I have come to see
The world in harmony.

- *Final Moments in an Indian Ashram*

Confident.
That's what they said I am.
 "Confident,"
 I said to myself in the bathroom mirror,
Feeling its alien sensation on my tongue.
A word I have never associated with myself before
But having heard my name next to it
Spinning like a playful puppy chasing its tail—
I know I am.

A person is given a fruit tree. Which fruit it will bear is a mystery. 'Maybe it's an apple tree,' they ponder, 'or an orange tree.' Despite their guesses, there is no way to know until it grows.

They take care of the tree to the best of their ability, watering it daily, protecting it from pests, and enriching the soil. Well cared for, the tree grows strong like a kid who drinks their milk. The caretaker tastes the decadence of a ripe cherry plucked from the branch and tastes the fruition of their hard work.

The possibility of the future is infinite. Nobody can say with absolute certainty what it holds. We only speculate. Don't pressure yourself to predict the unpredictable. If you invest yourself whole-heartedly in current passions— if you care for your tree— the future will blossom.

In my freshman English journal, I wrote that people often fear change, but it is life's greatest hope. If life stagnated, we cannot grow. Life is a cycle of flow and ebb ridden for self-betterment.

Conditions change, but the tide, through flow and ebb, is the same substance— water. Through the highs and lows of life, you are anchored to the deepest core of self. Believe in your resilience.

To my ninth-grade self and readers who find themselves in her company, do not drown in the rain. Take the umbrella of creative expression with you and you will brave any storm.

Made in the USA
Middletown, DE
10 April 2019